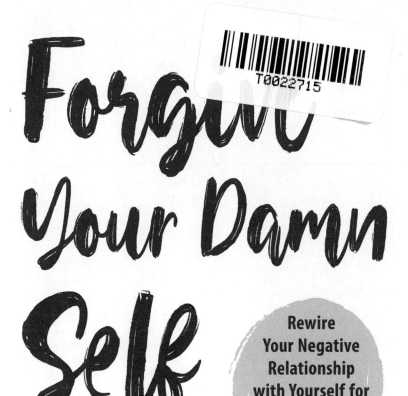

Forgive Your Damn Self

Rewire Your Negative Relationship with Yourself for More Positive Outcomes

GEORGIA MURCH

simple **truths**
Small books. BIG IMPACT.

Published by Simple Truths, an imprint of Sourcebooks
P.O. Box 4410, Naperville, Illinois 60567-4410
(630) 961-3900
sourcebooks.com

Originally published as *Flawsome* in 2020 in Australia by by Major Street Publishing.

Printed and bound in the United States of America.
SB 10 9 8 7 6 5 4 3 2 1

Contents

The Intro Bit

I've spent the last twelve years becoming known as the expert in designing feedback cultures in teams and organizations. It's been a passion project from the beginning, mainly born from a place of wanting the best conditions possible for people to thrive at work and home. But what I've increasingly seen and experienced—and witnessed in my own evolution—is that the feedback we give *ourselves* has a direct impact on how we speak and "be"—with ourselves as well as those around us.

The pursuit of being truly human is discombobulating. We are so damn tough on ourselves. Whether we're aware of it or not, we end up projecting how we feel about ourselves onto others. Our expectations of others rise and fall based on what we expect from ourselves.

My initial hypothesis was that in order to make peace with our humanity, we needed to drop our search for perfection.

We needed to be okay with being *enough*—flaws and all, no need for comparisons. At times, I've been able to achieve this, so I know it's a fabulous place to be, and I wanted to help others get to the same place. What I didn't realize is that achieving peace is actually far easier than we all think. The answer, I believe, is being flawsome.

Flawsome is being who you are. As coined by the amazing model and businesswoman Tyra Banks, it goes beyond making peace with your flaws; it means owning them, understanding them, and knowing that admitting them gives you power—it doesn't take your power away. Flawsome can be raw, hard, exposing, realigning, and reimagining (even when you feel like you are all out of imagination); it can undo you. But the work to embrace flawsome is absolutely worth it.

I thought the answer to inner peace would involve the feedback we give ourselves: what that is, how it needs to be rewired, what to believe, and what *not* to. But it's so much more. It's deeper. It has a ripple effect beyond measure and a timing without boundaries.

This book is for those who feel they need to use their abilities to be "enough" for others, that serving others makes them whole. (Being generous is a beautiful thing, but there's a better way.) It's for those who are capable in their field but still have a voice in their head that says, *Someone will find me out.* It's for those who are aware of their flaws and think they need to wrestle them down.

I assumed that as soon as we recognized and rewrote the stories of our past, we would be able to lead a flawsome life, that nature and nurture made us who we are. What I now know is that real freedom of heart, mind, and soul comes from living in alignment with who we are called to be.

You are not called to be an accountant, a speaker, or a cabinetmaker. You are called by a name—*your* name. You are called to be *you*, which could involve any number of roles. Knowing who *you* are and what being you truly means requires work. Just like growing into a new pair of sneakers, you need to grow into who you really are.

Life and experiences get in the way and tell us something different. Life tells us we need to win to be a winner, that no one will look out for us, so we need to become self-reliant. Life tells us we need to get great grades to have a great career and that a great career alone will make us happy.

And you know what? We all believed it to be true.

This book will help you rewrite those truths. Let's stop relying on beliefs that don't serve us. Let's not fake it till we make it. You can't be sustained on things that are not real and not true.

People ask me all the time, "Georgia, how do I *really* become a good leader/friend/parent/lover/human?" The "you already are" answer does not suffice here, and it's pretty unhelpful. So my answer is, "Do the work." This book will show you how.

Your challenge is to find the gold—for you. Seek out the content in this book that truly resonates, and take it as far as you like.

And then, of course, I'll welcome all the feedback. Especially the stuff that comes with love. ;-)

Are you ready to do the work? To forgive your damn self? What would that process entail for you?

_____

_____

_____

_____

_____

_____

_____

_____

_____

_____

THE INTRO BIT

_____

_____

_____

_____

_____

_____

_____

_____

_____

_____

_____

_____

_____

_____

_____

_____

_____

_____

_____

_____

_____

_____

_____

_____

PART I

The Pursuit of Flawsome

1

Learning to Be Holey

I first came across the word *flawsome* years ago when I heard it coined by Tyra Banks. Tyra is a supermodel and the creator and executive producer of *America's Next Top Model*. She is one of the pioneering African American supermodels following in the footsteps of Naomi Campbell in what was once a white-dominated industry. She became the first ever African American to be on the cover of the Victoria's Secret catalog and was a runway model for them until 2005. She has pushed against racism throughout her entire career, but that isn't all she's stood against.

During her career, Tyra was dropped from modeling and designer contracts after she put on some weight and was considered to be too curvy. Rather than starving herself and conforming to the industry standards, she decided to embrace her look and work with agencies that chose to do the same.

Tyra *stands* for being flawsome. Despite being a part of an industry that chases perfection, she chooses to celebrate her "flaws" and see them as what makes her awesome, to rejoice in her humanity and not hide from it. She decided that her aim wasn't perfection; it was distinction. How cool is that?

Not long after Tyra started producing *America's Next Top Model*, photos appeared in the tabloids showing her in a swimsuit with noticeable curves and cellulite. The photos were featured alongside an article titled "America's Next Top Waddle." She was working in an industry that expected and aimed for perfection, but this only spurred her on more. As a judge on the TV show, she taught women and men to highlight the things about themselves that were different from the "norm": Highlight your freckles, celebrate your curves, and love your nose that's bigger or teeth that have gaps between them. Make your flaws your own. Tyra is committed to helping everyone, especially young women, embrace their physical imperfections, such as weight fluctuations, unique facial features, and crooked teeth.

Tyra Banks and her flawsomeness got me thinking. If her legacy is about celebrating physicality in all its forms, why can't we do the same for our humanity? Why can't we choose to see the things about ourselves that we previously decided are not cool as unique parts of us—part of what makes us human and perfectly flawed?

Tyra taught me that being flawsome means accepting *all* of yourself. This doesn't mean you love all of yourself all of the time; being flawsome requires you to constantly reframe your thoughts, especially if, like me, you are starting to nudge your fifties, and bits are sagging that you never knew you had. But I am committed to my own evolution, and I am getting stronger at observing my judgment rather than latching onto it.

To be flawsome is to know that the things we think, what we look like, how we perform, and how we fail are part of who we are. Instead of hiding from our flaws, we own them. We wear them with less judgment and more understanding. We make friends with the parts of ourselves that we have typically judged as flaws, as holes in our selves, as bits that are missing or not right.

The journey to being whole is learning to be holey. To sit with who we are. To celebrate ourselves in all our holey-ness.

Honoring Your Cracks

Japan is an amazing country. I traveled there with my kids and good friends, the Laytons, for Christmas 2018. I was blown away by the kindness of the people, the incredible countryside, and the orderly and respectful way that millions and millions of people (who live pretty much on top of each other) make it work. The Japanese appreciate their culture and are very pragmatic about how they live. It's amazing what they can fit into small places and how resourceful they are. There are no trash cans on the streets, which forces people to take their trash with them when they leave places. Recycling is second nature for them; excessive consumption is not.

The Japanese have a practice known as *kintsukuroi*, which literally means "gold mending." It's a process that repairs broken objects, like cups and bowls, with gold. Instead of throwing objects away, they are repaired as well as beautified. According to art historians, the practice came about in the fifteenth century when a *shogun* (military leader) named Ashikaga Yoshimasa sent his favorite tea bowl to China to be repaired, and it came back stapled together. It was so poorly done that his local craftsmen were asked to repair it with a gold lacquer. They did a much better job, and the bowl looked unique and became more valuable. The repair turned a problem into a plus. The art of *honoring* broken things and highlighting the breaks instead of *hiding* them became a thing.

Imagine if we knew this principle when something about us was broken, or we discovered a crack (as we all do), that we would be given gold. Wouldn't we just want to find more flaws?

You'd have people lining up to declare their brokenness, right? (Okay, maybe that's too far, but you get my point.)

> **Hiding our flaws does not serve us, nor does it celebrate who we really are.**

If we didn't have these cracks, maybe we wouldn't be as valuable. To celebrate this is to honor ourselves and our humanity. Hiding our flaws does not serve us, nor does it celebrate who we really are.

What flaws do you need to face and fill with golden solutions?

_____

_____

_____

_____

_____

_____

_____

2

Your Flawsomeness Draws People to You

I used to avoid putting up videos of myself on social media. If we did decide to do a video—for example, to promote an event—I would leave it until the absolute last minute because I felt so uncomfortable. Eventually I would shoot the video, then have to redo it, then redo it again—the words weren't right, the angle was wrong, the tone wasn't exactly what I intended. It held us back. The market wanted to see short, quick sound bites, yet I was sticking to written blogs and newsletters because I wasn't "perfect" in videos. I made my perfection a greater priority than getting messages that could help others out to the market.

Then my good friend, author, and marketing strategist Brent Hodgson introduced me to the concept of the pratfall effect. A *pratfall* is a stupid or humiliating action—like when you fall on your backside in the middle of the street in front of everyone or get tongue-tied when you are speaking (or forget what you were saying altogether). When we experience this—as long as it's not *all* the time—our appeal to others *increases*. Yep, you're actually considered *more likable* when you make a blunder, as long as you have shown your credibility first.

Elliot Aronson first described the pratfall effect in 1966, and lots of studies have been performed since to prove the theory. One study looked at the likability and trust we have in doctors of psychiatry; it had observers compare doctors who spilled their coffee or dropped their pen (a physical pratfall) in their initial meeting with those who didn't. The results showed that people felt more drawn to those who made a mistake. The point is that when others make mistakes, we feel more sympathetic toward them; we get to see their human side.

> **Showing your vulnerability increases your connection with others.**

The pratfall effect supports the idea that if you want to build trust quickly with people, showing your flaws will help.

Showing your vulnerability *increases your connection* with others. This seemed like a Willy Wonka Golden Ticket to me. You mean I can cough, fall over my words, or even forget what I am saying for a second and still be taken seriously and make genuine connections? WTF? That is *revolutionary.* It meant that I had permission to be me—think light bulbs and fireworks. Learning about the pratfall effect completely changed how I approached communication. These days, I mostly create my videos in one take. I don't care if I make mistakes. It makes me flawsome!

The bottom line is that we don't easily trust people who seem too perfect, yet we live in a paradox where perfect is seen as better and anything less is failure. This is a trap. The pursuit of perfection is holding us back from connecting with others and ourselves—because we stay in judgment, not observation—and that can be an exhausting place to live.

> **We are drawn to people not for their perfection but for their acceptance of their imperfection.**

Where can you be vulnerable and show your true self to others? How will they be drawn to you?

3

An Unhealthy Relationship with Feedback

If you opened your email right now and saw a message with the subject, "I want to find a time to give you some feedback," what would you think? Honestly, what's your first gut reaction? If you're like most people, you will assume the worst. We are all a little cray-cray like that.

> **Inner peace is difficult to achieve when we are constantly anticipating the worst.**

We are wired to think in deficits. The technical term is a *negative bias*. Simply put, our brains have a greater sensitivity to negative news—to the point where we anticipate it. When we see good stuff, like videos of cute cats and incredible landscapes, we have a surge of stimuli in our brains. When we see pictures of starving children or hurt animals, there is an even greater surge of activity. We are wired like this to protect ourselves from danger—even if the danger is to our happiness. Our brains are trying to keep us out of harm's way. But inner peace is difficult to achieve when we are constantly anticipating the worst—especially if our worries are playing in our heads at an unhelpful volume.

This psychological phenomenon is why we tend to dwell on criticism or bad news: our brains respond to it at a greater level. It's why bad first impressions can be so hard to move on from and past traumatic events have such a lingering effect. Negativity stimulates us so much that we remember the feeling and don't want to experience it again, so we are on alert most of the time to avoid it.

We need to be conscious of how our brains work to decipher what is valuable to process and take on board from the feedback we receive and what is not. This will allow us to be open and not on edge. When we make peace with our flawsomeness, feedback will just become news: information that we can decide to learn from or put to the side. To know that we don't have to agree or disagree with information that comes toward us and that we can choose whether or not to receive feedback is the key.

Seth Godin, multiple bestselling author and the ultimate entrepreneur, is always a great source of pearls of wisdom. He says: "One piece of feedback is not the source of truth." He says we can skew our thinking based on the first piece of feedback we receive: "That's the moment of maximum fragility, and so our radar is on high alert." In other words, our stress radar is in action mode, so we might grip onto feedback—particularly feedback we receive early in a project or relationship—as if it's the truth. But remember: Feedback is just one perspective; it may be useful, or it may not. You get to decide.

Feedback is (1) information you receive and (2) how you respond to it. Both the receiving and responding are feedback: one is feedback that comes your way, and the other is feedback you give yourself.

Feedback is information we can choose to take on board and learn from or discard. It will always have the power to make us bitter or make us better. Motivational speaker Jay Shetty says, "Bitterness broods and better grows." I think he's 100 percent right. There is nothing to be gained from becoming frustrated at someone or the feedback they have given us; that eats us alive. Choosing to grow from the experience is a happier choice and one that serves us. The cool news is that we hold that power; we just need to learn how to use the power well. It's kind of like becoming a feedback Jedi.

Think of feedback you have been given in the past. Did you use it to make yourself bitter or better?

_____

_____

_____

_____

_____

_____

_____

_____

_____

_____

_____

_____

_____

_____

_____

_____

_____

_____

_____

4

It Starts with You

My good friend Lucas (one of my favorite humans) always says that you can't solve an internal problem with an external solution. I just love that. Lucas is very experienced in facing internal problems; he spent fifteen years as an addict. He tried everything under the sun to not only numb his emotional state but to try to find his happy. He and his wife, Erin, have now radically turned their lives around from addiction and destruction to serving the world around them in a very significant way. I have so much respect for them. He has been sober now for more than a decade and is one of the coolest guys I know.

Lucas often says that addiction is when your solution becomes your problem. However, addiction is not always about drugs and alcohol. For many of us, it could be an unhealthy obsession with pleasing others, staying in a destructive relationship, or pursuing physical perfection.

We need to be careful that our medication doesn't become our disease. We need to create awareness so we are not welcoming distractions or substitutions that become a new pain for us to work through or shed.

If you are uncomfortable with your own thoughts and feelings, do you spend time on social media to distract yourself? Powerful data is proving that anxiety and depression increase when we compulsively use social media. Do you self-medicate by being super busy? If so, you are probably exhausted because you are doing too much. When we self-medicate, we often find ourselves with a new problem to solve—but the old one hasn't gone away either.

You can't fail at one relationship and move to another thinking it will automatically be better. We throw food out when it is past its expiration date; why don't we do the same for our unhealthy thinking patterns and behaviors that don't serve us?

Making peace with who you are—with all your lumps and bumps, highs and lows, and strengths and weaknesses—is being flawsome. Hiding from these things by replacing them with unhealthy habits only slows you down, and ultimately your quest for joy and happiness will fail.

It's not about high performance. Flawsome is about high acceptance, irrespective of whether you meet a goal or not.

We also can't expect the world, and all the people in it, to bend to our way of doing life or to work around us so we can get what we need. Not only is this an impossible expectation, but at its core, it is very self-focused; it is saying that my way is *the* way, and you all need to change for me.

I get it though. If only others spoke less so we could get a word in. Or maybe they could contribute more and do their part. If only they could speak with kindness or be less emotional. Whatever it may be that you need others to do more or less of, expecting this is still a form of control. You're saying, "When you change, I can be more or better, and life will be easier." But the other person must do all the work; it's a transfer of responsibility and a form of blame. Ouch, right?

We can't expect others to change for us to be at peace. You can't make others see you as important. You can't do someone else's learning for them. This is not your role.

To achieve inner peace, we think we need our colleagues, our friends, or our families to act differently, to speak differently, to just *be* different. That's like asking someone else to go to the hairdresser for you.

We have to do the work. We must work to understand what's going on, our reactions to it, how we can learn from it, and then rewire to be better. It starts with how we respond in situations with people we love and those whom we struggle to love. We can learn from people we know deeply and even those we've just met or even never will. Every person and circumstance provides an opportunity to learn and grow, yet we push these learning opportunities away.

> **It's not about high performance. Flawsome is about high acceptance, irrespective of whether you meet a goal or not.**

We can learn about ourselves through our everyday interactions. Did you judge the Uber driver when you hopped in the car or before they were even there? Did you find yourself being short? Did you treat them as a human being or as a service? Every interaction is an opportunity to learn.

What about how you are with your family? Now that's a trigger for many people, and sometimes it feels like there is no learning to be had. But these interactions can be unopened gifts—a bit like gold. Gold is hard to find—you have to search for special places in the earth and the sea to source it. But when you do find it, it's very valuable. Finding the gift in your experiences with others can feel like that too.

Where in your world are you asking or expecting another person to change to make your world easier? Who are you blaming?

5

Finding Your Evolution

If we want to start understanding ourselves, part of the journey is learning about how we connect and react to things around us. If we ignore this opportunity, we are just an island. An island cannot sustain itself for the long term; it eventually needs other resources and the land to be tended for it to continue to survive. We need other people, who become our fuel, to live well.

The ultimate flawsome state is one where we never stop learning and growing, and we accept that this is the best way to be. It means we are in a permanent state of evolution. Evolution doesn't have an end date; it keeps going to infinity. Any information that comes our way—whether it's what we tell ourselves or what we learn from others—is just that: information. It's something to understand, look at, and learn from.

There may be some spaces in your life where you feel you are in a permanent state of growth, and you are aware of what is happening and able to suspend judgment of both others and yourself. However, most of us are always wavering in our learning. Some days are great, some are not. In some moments, we excel, and in others, we react poorly. That's okay. The journey to flawsome is not linear; it ebbs and flows. It's your intention that's important.

Let's look at some of the phases we can move in and out of to grow into a state of evolution.

OUR INTENT	OUR STATE	OUR GROWTH		
With awareness	Comes evolution	∞	From a place of surrender	ABOVE THE LINE
With forgiveness	Comes acceptance	+100		
With ownership	Comes regulation	+10	From a place of responsibility	
With denial	Comes disconnection	-50	From a place of domination	BELOW THE LINE
With blame	Comes assassination	-100		

You can see that there are "above the line" and "below the line" growth patterns. You may have heard about this as an accounting concept used to track revenue and expenses. In the marketing field, it is also used as a market segmentation tool. In our case, it's about ourselves.

Being *above the line* is about staying open and curious and responding well because your intention comes from a good place. Below the line is when you are closed, defending, or protecting—defending yourself either passively or explicitly and denying you have a role to play. It's about avoidance of responsibility.

When you are not in growth, you are likely to have a strong relationship with control, which is about dominating others and your thinking (being your own God). You decide who is right and wrong, and you blame others for your situation—coming from a place of domination. This is a below-the-line state. *Domination* can look like trying to control your environment, your workplace rules, and the people around you. It's when we need the people and things around us to change for us to be okay or when we deny what is really going on. If you find yourself not wanting to accept the circumstances you find yourself in or pretending things are not happening, you're probably in a below-the-line state.

When you start noticing how you are responding to the outside world and decide to respond in a positive way, you move into responsibility. This is where you manage your responses, understanding that there is a better way and that you must self-regulate.

The opposite of domination is *surrender*. To surrender is to observe how people are behaving and what is happening in our world and to know what we can influence and what we can leave. Surrender is a place where we know the only person we can control is ourselves, and therefore it comes from a place of love and self-acceptance. Surrender takes not just awareness but vulnerability.

All of these phases that we move in and through come from intent. We may or may not be conscious of our intent, but either way, it has an impact—it influences how we connect to and respond to others and with ourselves.

So let's explore each phase and see if we can self-assess where we tend to land. Once you know where you stand, you can define what you need to do in order to reach your ultimate flawsome state.

We will start at the bottom of the ladder to learn about our unhelpful behaviors and what causes them to grow within us.

Blame Breeds Assassination

I've been practicing yoga for more than fifteen years now. I started not long after having my second child, Holly. I've learned a lot about myself from yoga. At the start, I would get so annoyed and frustrated at myself for not getting into a pose or being able to hold it; at the heat (keep in mind I chose to go to Bikram yoga, which is 104°F and forty poses); and at the teachers for not being clear enough, strong enough, or kind enough.

I remember this one teacher; we will call her Tina. Tina was a strong woman—physically and, I presumed, psychologically. I attended a lot of Tina's classes, and over time, her style really started to grate on me. Her instructions were always very clear and precise. Her encouragement, when we got the pose correct, was generous. But when we didn't get the pose right or we needed a rest, it was obvious that she was not impressed. If the class was struggling to keep the pace or strength *that she expected*, she would often stop the class and make a statement. Some examples: "Am I teaching the elderly class today?" or "Is that the best you've got?" Sometimes she would just laugh out loud and ask people to guess why she was laughing.

Lots of people liked her classes. She was strong and taught a strong class. She cracked gags and would often share a little anecdote. I, however, decided her comments were passive-aggressive and that she was trying to shame us into submission. I decided she was wrecking my practice. When I went to the class and saw she was the teacher, I would do an internal sigh and have to self-manage myself through the class. This went on for a couple of years.

Then one day, I started learning about projection. I learned that the things we react to in others are often a reflection of our own behaviors. *Ouch!* Many of these behaviors exist in the shadows, that is, they are not easy to see. We blame or punish others for the things we don't like in ourselves. It's quite subconscious too.

Austrian neurologist Sigmund Freud first spoke of projection and then worked with psychiatrist Carl Jung to further develop the theory. Together they explored what happens when your ego is not willing to see certain parts of yourself. These days, there are a lot of experts in this space. One of my favorites is Byron Katie. The work she does to help people unlock what's getting in the way of them being their best is not about shame or blame, nor is it about proving who is right and who is wrong. As she says in *Loving What Is*, "The power of the turnaround lies in the discovery that everything you think you see on the outside is really a projection of your own mind. Everything is a mirror image of your own thinking."

So if you start becoming aware of what you see in others as a projection of yourself, you hold the key to your own evolution; you have the power to see or not to see. How cool is that?

Well, if I applied the theory of projection to how I felt about Tina, what then? My first reaction was to think, *OMG! I can't be passive-aggressive, can I?* But when I dug deeper, I realized that, *Yep, passive-aggressive is my default when I don't like what other people are doing or saying.* It was tough to realize and process through.

Blame is the discharge of truth. We need to understand the role blame plays in our lives. When we blame, we shut our minds off to possibility. Blame becomes an excuse to avoid seeing another's perspective. I'm not suggesting here that everyone is without faults. What I mean is, if you learn to stand in other people's shoes rather than blaming them, you might begin to understand their perspective. It doesn't mean you have to agree with everything they say and think, but you will have empathy. It will be easier for you to learn and for others to be with you.

Blame is binary thinking: yes or no, good or bad. Blaming others isn't helpful, but neither is self-blame. And we can all fall into this habit easily.

Who, or what, are you blaming right now for how you respond?

_____

_____

_____

_____

_____

_____

_____

_____

_____

_____

_____

_____

_____

_____

_____

_____

_____

We "Should" All over Ourselves

As part of the research for this book, I interviewed hundreds of people. The questions focused on what "giving yourself permission to be human" means and how much permission people give themselves. I also asked about the state of people's self-talk and actions when they are in a good space and when they are also in a bad space. The hypothesis that I had at the start was that people would tell me that their pursuit of perfection was getting in the way of them giving themselves permission to be "enough," that their flaws held them back. There were instances of this, but it was not the resounding theme.

Most suggested that allowing yourself to be human is about permission to be messy, to fail, and to show weakness; being okay with not meeting expectations—your own and others'; giving yourself a break; and not being emotional when you make mistakes.

A smaller proportion said allowing yourself to be human is being brave enough to be who you really are—your authentic self; to know that you are a work in progress and always will be; to be real with yourself and others; and to realize that we are multidimensional beings.

The really interesting part is that over 70 percent of people asked me whether they should answer my questions in a work or life context. Others self-selected to talk about themselves in a work context. I did not expect the research to go one way or the other or for people to be so definitive about the difference. This was an interesting surprise. It showed me that people see themselves as playing a role in a work environment, whereas in their private lives, they are more comfortable with being themselves.

> **The person we take to work is also the person we take home.**

Think about yourself like an orange. Whether you put that orange on the boardroom table, in the local coffee shop, or at home in the kitchen, it's still an orange; the inside stays the same. It's the same for you.

The 70 percent of people who questioned the context of my interviews believed they were not supported in a work environment to be who they truly are, to show their humanity. It's still about permission, right? Permission to be who you really are— the at-home version of yourself.

It got me thinking: What holds people back from giving themselves permission to be who they really are, especially at work? One of the big reasons, I believe, is that we "should" all over ourselves. My interviewees made these sorts of comments:

"I *should* have known that was going to happen."

"I *should* have worked harder or smarter."

"I *should* have achieved more by now."

"I *should* have been around more for the kids or my partner."

"I *should* have reacted differently."

"I *should* have said nothing, done nothing."

Interestingly, the more experience people had, the louder the voice became: "I'm such an idiot. I'm so stupid." We are more experienced in self-punishing than self-approving. When we believe we *should have* known better, it is driven from a place of shame. It serves no one, but it's a common space we play in.

Where in your world are you asking or expecting another person to change to make your world easier? Where are you blaming another or a circumstance for being wrong because you are right? Where is your thinking binary and fixed?

Or are you in self-blame and "shoulding" all over yourself? When do you tell yourself you should have known better, should have done better, or should be better? Assassination of others and of self becomes the result. Blame breeds assassination.

When do you "should" all over yourself and have expectations of the way you should or shouldn't be?

_____

_____

_____

_____

_____

_____

_____

_____

_____

_____

_____

_____

_____

_____

_____

_____

_____

_____

Denial Breeds Disconnection

Here's the funny thing about denial: you might not admit you are in it or even be able to name it, but deep down, something won't feel right. I love how my friend James Layton talks about denial. He says it's like walking around with poo on your shoe thinking someone else stinks. How good is that?

Why do people linger in denial then? I can't presume to know anyone's exact reasons, but it will always come from a foundation of fear. Fear comes in many forms: fear of having to confront parts of yourself that you do not like; fear of learning about those around you and the role you have let them play in your life; fear of having to take responsibility for the role you have played in your own life. Denial becomes a place where people can feel safe.

People in denial downplay the impact of other people or situations in their life. People who are highly defensive can be in denial that there is some truth in another's words. People who refuse to admit that they played a role in the failure of a relationship, a role, or a decision are also in denial. (Stay with me. Don't go into denial now.)

The human brain is an incredible thing. It has the ability to reframe a situation, whether it serves us or not. This is called *neuroplasticity*. The term was first used by Polish neuroscientist Jerzy Konorski in 1948 to describe how the neurons (cells) in the brain can change. The research morphed in the 1960s to show that the brain not only responds but can reorganize itself, for good or bad.

> **No matter who you are, your brain
> has developed coping mechanisms
> to help you deal with life.**

Coping mechanisms can be helpful or unhelpful. When our brains have an unhealthy response, it can become hard for us to address the real issues or make behavioral changes. It's basically a coping mechanism—we are blocking events or words from our conscious awareness. If there is something we don't want to address or that feels too hard to cope with (especially when traumatic circumstances are involved), we simply refuse to accept it and sometimes even remember it. We pretend it's not real and therefore doesn't have an impact on us.

It's like when your body goes into a coma to keep itself alive. Your mind does the same. It shuts out what it needs to in order to cope. Fear-based memories or traumatic experiences can sometimes lead to avoidance behaviors that can hold you back from living life to the fullest.

I have been told over the years, many times, that I can be intimidating. This feedback hasn't come from people of a particular gender, age, or seniority—it seems it was people's experience of me across the board. For years, I honestly believed that people were just coming from a place of their own insecurity, that they needed to be stronger and "less sensitive."

In my heart, I believed that you should be strong and speak your "truth" and that other people should be open to hear it. This stance meant that it took me a long, long time to rewire my thinking. I was open to hearing other people's perspective of me, but I didn't believe what they were saying. On the other hand, if someone else intimidated me, did I believe they needed to soften or adapt their style? *Abso-friggin-lutely.*

The crunch came one year when I felt like I received a barrage of feedback about my style. I had taken on more responsibility, and therefore more accountability, at work, and what I have learned over my career and after working with thousands of leaders is that the more you take on, the more people expect of you. That's just the way leadership works.

With my role growing, so too did others' expectations of me. Suddenly, the way I spoke to people and treated them was in the spotlight. I was told I could be short with people and was sometimes dismissive. I was told I gave a particular "look" when it appeared I didn't like what people were saying. I was also told that I cut people off and discounted their opinions.

Well, f*** me. The person they were describing was not the person I believed I was. But I also knew that awareness is a combination of what you believe *and* how others perceive you. *Boom!* Hit the pain button. The pain of realizing you are not the leader, or the person, you thought you were, that you've got work to do and that people avoid you, is tough to feel.

But I knew if I didn't feel it and take the feedback on board, I would stay in my bubble of denial. Staying in denial meant I *could not* grow.

I have stayed in denial in a few past relationships too. I was in denial when a person I was with had very few close friends; I told myself that it was gorgeous that he wanted to be with me 24/7 because he loved me to bits. I ignored his jealousy and denied it would become a problem.

The thing about denial is that it is hard to see. You can see it in others easily, but it's much harder to spot in yourself. The good news is that we can all tap into our internal denial radar if we really try. Our bodies can detect when things aren't right, even when they appear so. Gut feel is a real thing. Have you ever noticed that feeling of nausea in your stomach when someone asks you to do something that is outside your comfort zone? Maybe you've noticed those butterflies in your tummy when you are about to meet someone who excites you, or the subtle and unexplainable feeling when something just isn't *right*.

Those feelings that sometimes have no logical explanation are your gut feelings or intuition. We're all familiar with the concept, but are we all on top of how to actually apply it and use it?

We now know that the gut and the brain are connected and that this connection goes both ways. The brain can affect the gut, specifically a stressed or anxious brain can cause digestive and stomach issues. Think about those moments we spend on the toilet before having to do a presentation or ruminating over *that* conversation. The gut can also affect the brain. We all have neurotransmitters that go directly from our brains to our guts. The gut has even been described as the second brain.

Our brains recall every decision, every meeting, every interaction, every conversation—whether it's conscious or unconscious. They store a vast amount of information that we are not inherently aware of. It's like a jigsaw puzzle, and the only pieces we have within our immediate reach are those we are conscious of.

It makes sense that as we gather more experiences in life and understand and reflect on what our intuitions told us in past situations, we are able to hone our intuitions. If we make the space to reflect and learn, we can refine this tool. So when your intuition speaks, listen to it. Don't ignore it. Investigate it. Be aware of it. I'm not saying you should make all your decisions based on gut feelings alone; if you don't have any facts or examples to prove your thinking, one way or the other, then be careful. However, I am suggesting that your intuition is something that needs to be explored and understood.

Are there any parts of your life that your gut tells you could be worthwhile to explore? Is there anything you are adamant about that others tell you that you could be incorrect about? Do you suspect there could be another way of thinking about something you feel strongly about? It's worth exploring. If you're not prepared to do the work to explore your potential areas of denial, you might be creating a disconnection with yourself and pushing away those around you. It might be lonely, and there's another way—a better way to live and be. Denial breeds disconnection.

What feedback have you received in the past that did not resonate? Could you be in a little bit of denial?

_____

_____

_____

_____

_____

_____

_____

_____

_____

_____

_____

_____

_____

_____

_____

_____

_____

_____

_____

_____

_____

_____

_____

_____

Ownership Breeds Regulation

Taking responsibility for the impact you have requires a level of maturity and bravery. It's saying, "I am aware of the role I play in others' lives and the impact I might have both on them and myself." It's owning it; it's like putting your grown-up pants on.

These days, I own the fact that I may intimidate people. I take responsibility for when I am short with my kids, my work colleagues, and people on the street. I know that I can shut down when I am with someone who presses my buttons and that this might come across as me being disinterested. This doesn't mean I have transformed into love, light, and happiness, but I am much more aware of my behavior and how it affects others.

> Sometimes it's really hard to
> accept the impact we have on those
> around us and ourselves.

We become ashamed of our behavior, and it feels painful. Sometimes we are willing to accept some things about ourselves, but other things still stay on the shelf—that ol' denial popping its head up again. Regulating how you respond is self-control. That's a good thing; it's management of self. When you know how to do that, you make it easy for others to be around you. You also make yourself open to learning.

I know that when I am stressed or put into situations I find taxing, I need to be careful not to lash out or say something I regret. My natural response is to fight the situation or the person. I know I need to self-regulate during those times and not be passive-aggressive (or even just plain aggressive). I realize I must stay open to the other person's perspective and be careful of my need to win or be right.

Others might fall into flight behaviors and just want to avoid the person, the conversation, or the circumstance. If this is you, you have to own this and self-manage to stay in the conversation. Flighters might fall in the trap of passive agreement;

that is, they say "Yes, whatever you want," to avoid the conflict. Flighters need to be conscious of creating passive agreement, where they agree to what the others say to avoid the conversation or shut down altogether. Fighters need to replace being right with being curious. Flighters need to replace an exit strategy with an entry strategy.

Think about someone in your life, past or present, who always appears calm under pressure. When they get bad news or someone disagrees with them, they remain in control. What we don't know is whether this is coming from a place of self-control or if they are genuinely not affected by another's behavior. By taking responsibility and self-managing, it is possible for us to remain still and controlled even in situations that disturb us.

The thing about responsibility is that it is freeing. It means we own our parts. It means we are moving from being a toddler, who is unaware of how they connect with and impact others, to being a grown-up and taking responsibility for our actions by self-regulating.

This goes back to why we often say we are different at work than we are at home. Usually, it's because we exercise more self-control at work because we don't feel as safe to be ourselves. Here's the thing: self-management all the time can be tiring, because it is coming from a place of management—it's not a natural response. Yet we know it's a mature one. Ownership breeds regulation.

Are there circumstances in your world where you know you self-manage rather than react naturally? Are there people who you know who require some deep breaths before you connect with them? The good news is that there is an easier place to operate from that will allow you to be with those people and ultimately with yourself. It's about forgiveness.

Where are you currently taking ownership of the impact you have on those around you?

_____

_____

_____

_____

_____

_____

_____

_____

_____

_____

_____

_____

_____

_____

_____

Forgiveness Breeds Acceptance

I've been going to Narcotics Anonymous (NA) meetings to support one of my dear friends. She hit a milestone in her recovery, which was ninety days clean. It was incredibly special to be there and see her celebrated; she received her ninety-day chip for getting through one of the toughest experiences of her life.

For those of you who are not aware of what an NA meeting involves, in essence it creates a space where people can openly process where they are at. They are given the chance to share what's going on for them for up to five minutes, with no judgment and no advice. They can just be whatever they like and say whatever they want. And they do. It's real and raw.

The theme for this particular meeting was the Twelve Steps. The Twelve Steps is a set of guiding principles providing a road map for recovery from addiction. Members of this particular meeting were asked to reflect on the impact of the Twelve Steps on their recovery. I noticed that people kept referring to Step 4—"Make a searching and fearless moral inventory of ourselves"—as being one of the toughest to move through. This step is apparently the one that people can get consistently stuck on; at worst, it could throw people back to using again.

What is Step 4 really asking? It's about doing a deep and personal—and often confronting—inventory of who we really are and our past and current behaviors. It means being ruthlessly honest about where we are at and have been. I can see why this caused some people to get stuck.

When we do things we are not proud of, make decisions that don't serve us or those around us, or dislike (or even hate and loathe) traits about ourselves, we often live in shame. The thing about shame is that it is secretive. We hide these feelings and thoughts, and it can be extremely uncomfortable to wrestle with and understand them.

What the members of NA are learning, in the meetings and via Step 4, is to understand the antidote to shame: shine a light on our darker thoughts and feelings that we are not proud of. When we acknowledge and start to understand our flaws, shame has nowhere to hide. Vulnerability is the antidote to shame. Brené Brown nails it in *Daring Greatly* when she says:

> Vulnerability sounds like truth and feels like courage. Truth and courage aren't always comfortable, but they're never weakness. Because true belonging only happens when we present our authentic, imperfect selves to the world, our sense of belonging can never be greater than our level of self-acceptance.

The thing about forgiveness is that it is not a gift for another person: it's your gift. It means you can move forward and release the angst and burden that you've been holding on to. Forgiveness of self is the harder one to accomplish.

We love a bit of self-flagellation, don't we? Even if we don't physically harm ourselves, we can self-flagellate in our minds. We ruminate on our wrongs; most of us have an ever-present enemy that sits on our shoulders and whispers (or yells) in our ears. Guilt is the emotion that drives our need to beat up on ourselves for what we are ashamed of having done or are doing or didn't do that we should have done. The more guilty we feel, the less able we are to forgive ourselves.

The perfectionists among us really have it bad. They are stricken with guilt because everything they do is not as perfect as it "should" be. Then there are those of us who tend to worry about what others might think, even when we are doing what is right for ourselves. That's not so much a question of guilt as it is shame; it's a lack of feelings of worth.

Of course, guilt and shame are closely related. Guilt comes from our actions or behaviors, but if what we do makes us feel ashamed of who we are, then shame is added to the guilt. Shame is related to who we are as people: "I did something wrong; therefore, I am a bad person."

I connect with Colin Tipping in his book *Radical Self-Forgiveness*:

> Once we recognize that what we see and criticize in others is simply a reflection of what we can't stand in ourselves, it becomes clear that we are being given an opportunity to heal the split within ourselves. By taking back all our projections and loving the parts of us we had previously hated, we expand into love for ourselves and return ourselves to wholeness.

Learning to be okay with where we are at and learning from our experiences is the next step. This is flawsome. And it requires forgiveness, including forgiveness of self—one of the hardest things to do.

Forgiveness facilitates a place where we stop needing to

control ourselves and those around us and practice the art of surrendering: surrendering to what's happened and accepting it. To get to a place of self-acceptance, you need to start with loving yourself in all your flawsomeness. Forgiveness is the start. Forgiveness breeds acceptance.

What do you need to forgive yourself for to make peace with your flawsomeness?

Awareness Breeds Evolution

Awareness is an incredible state. It comes from a place where your eyes are wide open to the possibilities of self, others, and new ideas. In a state of awareness, you can see how you react to yourself and others and learn from it. Getting into this state requires us to drop our aims and expectations.

Sometimes awareness comes easily because we are not attached to an outcome; we are open to what will be. Let's be real though: it might not always be effortless. Being open means accepting the pain and discomfort that comes with it. It requires energy and bravery. But once you are aware, you will no longer feel like a cat chasing its tail. Awareness is not fruitless; it allows you to see the things that need to be seen—in both yourself and the world around you.

Awareness sees that you might hurt someone with your words, but it doesn't judge you. It is wise, so it will propel you to go and offer an apology if one is needed.

My friend Annie and I have known each other since we were teenagers—in the days when perms and shoulder pads were cool. The minute we met, we were tight. The quality I adore about this woman, among other things, is her commitment to her own evolution. She is dedicated to growing, learning, and developing. She has also done the work to understand who she is, find her identity, and learn to surrender.

Annie's evolution hasn't always been pretty. Understanding yourself and taking responsibility for who you are is often a rocky road. It involves rewriting stories you have told yourself that are not true, asking for forgiveness from others, and forgiving yourself. It's knowing that what you are saying or doing has a ripple effect. Annie does not shy away from that process. She does the work, and she inspires me to do the same. For eight years, with her husband, James, she led a church called Encore. Encore's motto was "Cheering you on no matter where you are at." It evolved into a place where their people were encouraged to live in a state of awareness, to accept themselves and one another as they are and know that we all have work to do. It was truly an accepting place. (Yes, there are churches that discourage judgment, believe it or not.)

So how do you know if you're in a state of awareness? For me, it's when someone has a differing opinion to me and I recognize the reaction I'm having. Awareness doesn't mean you are no longer of this world and should start wearing a robe or cape. It means you see your fight or flight responses. It means you are also open to other perspectives. You want to hear others' views and learn from them and about yourself in the process.

You know you are in awareness when you can see yourself retreating from a situation or conversation and you are driven to question and understand why. It's when you recognize your desire to self-sabotage yet feel drawn to finding another, healthier way. When you do or say something that doesn't serve you or others and you don't self-assassinate—that's self-awareness. You notice your mistakes, own them without beating yourself up, and learn from them—either at the time or later. Awareness is cheering yourself on no matter where you are at.

You might ask yourself, "Why can't I just learn to be a beautiful mess? Why does mess have to be good or bad—why can't it just *be*?" The answer is that the journey to flawsome is not linear. There will be people and areas in your life that will be harder to crack. But moving to a state of awareness and evolution can only be achieved when, as Plato and Socrates put it, you "know thyself."

Your evolution is, simply put, having the courage to be open to another truth. It's to understand that you are perfectly imperfect and that without an awareness of your flaws, you are not being real. Know that awareness breeds evolution.

If you truly accepted who you are, how would you love and lead better?

_____

_____

6

The Path to Flawsome

If you have been reading this looking for a checklist of things you need to do and say to become flawsome, sorry—I ain't got one. That's because I don't know you. Heck, *you* probably don't even properly know you. But every person has their own path to acceptance and love. That said, I do have some key principles that I have found helpful, gleaned from my more than a decade of studying evolution of self and the role our reactions to feedback play in helping us grow.

The feedback you give yourself and the information you gather from those you connect or disconnect with can be used as your superpower. It can help you grow and develop as a leader, a partner, and a friend. The three components I bring to you here will help you understand how you can learn from every moment, every interaction, and every conversation you have with others and yourself. This can set you up for an incredible journey of self-knowing and, ideally, self-loving.

Let's explore these three principles to go on the ride to becoming flawsome. You will notice they are cyclical: they can happen in order but are much more likely to happen all at once. However, just like learning a new language, I suggest you start with one thing at a time.

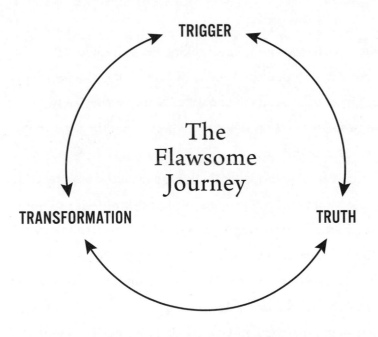

UNDERSTAND YOUR TRIGGERS

Have you ever played a character in a play? Or been in a band or part of a group presentation? For you to play your role, you would have been looking for a cue from someone else. Whether the cue was a phrase, a look, or a movement, you would have waited for it to indicate that it was your turn to play your role.

Identifying the things that trigger you is the same. But if you don't know what to look for, you won't get to learn about the role you play when the trigger occurs, nor will you know how to respond in a way that helps rather than hinders.

SEEK THE TRUTH

The truth is tricky. What's the truth in conversations or situations? Is it what you say or another person's perspective? Maybe it's a combination of both or neither.

The reconciliation of what you believe about yourself and the impact you have on others is where you learn. We need to remain open to whatever is coming our way. If we treat feedback as information, the learning begins. When we react poorly, we stifle our opportunity to grow. Your search for truth lies in curiosity and observation.

At a simple level, what you know to be true plus what others know lays the foundation for learning. Learning to meet in the middle and let the truth in (even when it's painful) is where the magic begins. It's fear that holds us back from being open, fear that what others say or make us feel could be true.

CONTINUE YOUR TRANSFORMATION

Transformation sits in courage: your courage to be open to many truths, to know that one perspective of you is just that. It's not automatically adopting others' beliefs but pondering the information and seeing it as an opportunity to add to what you already know and see. The aim is to add to your pool of truth, not diminish it.

Transformation is endless. It requires discomfort, to know that you are perfectly flawed.

Even when you own being flawsome, will there still be times when you don't like what you see or hear? Yep. Will there still be times when you feel low or inadequate? Probably, because you're human and perfectly flawed. But what I can guarantee is that if you keep getting back up again and continue to apply these three principles, you will get stronger and better each time. I know this because I've done the work myself, and I will keep doing it forever. I am committed to my evolution; it's never-ending.

Are you ready to shift into a life made flawsome?

What triggers do you need to be aware of as you shift into a life made flawsome?

PART II

Your Transformation

7

Now for Your Transformation

Transformation is a word that tends to be thrown around flippantly. Organizations claim to be going through transformational programs; people go on retreats to transform into new people; teams go on offsites to transform into high performers. But how often are these attempts at transformation actually successful?

Transformation is not a destination; it's an evolution into infinity. It also takes time. If transformation could happen in a single weekend, we'd all subscribe to those retreats. We'd fork out thousands of dollars knowing we would emerge as a new person, team, or business. (In fact, many of us *do* fork out money like that, yet we don't get the results we expect.)

Transformation is a profound journey that evolves over

time. Sometimes it appears as a big *aha* moment or event, but it mostly takes shape in the small moments. The irony of it is that it's about surrendering to what is happening and trying to understand it rather than control it.

We can't manufacture our own evolution; it happens in its own time, and it is not as illustrious or unobtainable as you may think. If you put in the work to take responsibility for your triggers, understand the real truth behind them, and make them mean something that serves you, you will transform. It is that simple and that profound.

Be Like a Butterfly

The year 2019 was significant for me. At the beginning of the year, I felt like I was permanently walking through mud, and it didn't smell or taste pleasant. My gorgeous kids, Jacko and Holly, went from behaving like relatively normal teenagers (grunting, talking back, self-focused) to being next-level teenagers (getting stuck into things they shouldn't, riddled with anxiety, skipping school). They are both very different humans, and I don't want to share the details (that's their story to tell if they choose), but needless to say, it was tough—particularly given they split their time between me and their dad.

At the same time, I was offered the project of a lifetime. I redesigned my business around it to make sure I could take it on, but then the opportunity was withdrawn. On top of that, I received a fair bit of feedback about my style from people I respect, and I was coming to terms with the fact that I had even more work to do on myself. This hurt, because it forced me to reconcile the fact that the person I want to be is not always the one that comes across. Fark!

I experienced health challenges; hormonal changes gave me night sweats, ridiculous emotional roller coasters, and foggy brain. My dad's health was quickly declining. And to top it off, many of my close friends had moved away. It felt like life was coming at me from all angles.

One night in particular, I became quite overwhelmed. I went for a walk around my local streets. I cried it out. Crying is good: it releases hormones that can reduce your anxiety, and it slows your heart rate and your breathing. That's why we sometimes experience a mood boost at the end of a good cry.

After my little mood-boosting cry, I decided the only way forward was to surrender control of everything that was happening to me. Depending on your beliefs, you might surrender to the universe, to Mother Nature, to God, or to just the world in general. I decided that I didn't want to attach my feelings to a particular outcome—whether it be to do with the kids, my dad, my career, or even my health. I was choosing to ditch any expectations I had of the outcomes.

I realized that attaching a preconceived idea of how I wanted (and, in some cases, needed) things to work out ended up creating more stress for me—and those around me. That's because this behavior is grounded in control: control of what the outcome should be and how I should feel about it. I wanted less of *that*. I wanted to focus on living life, being good enough, and doing just enough without expecting things to work out in a particular way. I wanted to become agnostic about the future of my actions.

Serendipitously, during this time, I was also consistently drawn to butterflies.

I saw them in my dreams, in magazines I picked up, and scattered throughout my social media feeds. I even saw someone doing a keynote about the butterfly's life cycle. This prompted me to do some research; whenever I see so many coincidences in life, it's often a sign that I need to look into it.

I found out that we can learn a lot from the butterfly. They start out as a genderless caterpillar when they wriggle around all fuzzy and cute. Then one day, they stop eating, hang themselves upside down on a twig or leaf, and spin into a silky cocoon. They become a chrysalis. And here's the really cool (and kinda gross) part: they end up eating themselves. If you cut into one at just the right time, you would see a caterpillar "soup" mixture ooze out. This protein-rich soup starts to form the cells of the butterfly.

The whole soup can start with fifty cells and finish with up to fifty thousand.

Once this metamorphosis is complete, he or she (now gender specific) transforms into a beautiful butterfly. The butterfly is hardwired to transform. Without transformation, it can't reproduce, since the caterpillar egg is laid by a butterfly. Their evolution, for survival, is imperative. Unlike butterflies, we humans are soft-wired. We can choose to transform or not.

For me, 2019 felt like the butterfly's journey. At the start of the year, I felt like everything I knew to be true was changing, and I was walking around in a haze. I felt like I was eating myself. I had become trapped in trying to control my life and the things around me so that I could feel better. But the problem was, while I could control myself and my reactions, I couldn't control my kids, my family, my team, my health, or my career. I could influence them, but that's all.

The beauty of living through times in your life when things feel overwhelming is that you are just on the other side of transformation. When you surrender, you can transform and "eat" your old beliefs that don't serve you. You become more beautiful; you can fly. But you need to trust the process.

The concept of transformation of self is not unique to the butterfly. In Buddhism, reaching *enlightenment* is a form of transformation. The ultimate state is nirvana. *Nirvana* is when you end suffering of self and others. In Christianity, we can be "born again" into a renewed mind and spirit. Eckhart Tolle describes enlightenment as "an egoless state." He says it is not something you can plan to achieve in the future; you must look at your present state.

When Our Transformations Are Interrupted

If you interrupt the formation of a chrysalis, a butterfly will never form. Yet if our evolution is interrupted, it doesn't mean we don't transform. In fact, that very interruption could be part of our evolution. We just don't know it yet.

We can subconsciously interrupt our own transformations by being too busy, endlessly scrolling social media, drinking, taking drugs, or working beyond our given capacity. If we blame someone else for the pain or frustration we are feeling, we are hijacking our own evolution. It pays to remember the stories we tell ourselves:

"If I don't do this, then no one else will."

"If she hadn't broken my heart, then I wouldn't be in this place."

"If they did their part, I wouldn't need to work all these hours."

Any of these sound familiar?

Sometimes we can defend the very beliefs that are eating us alive. We get stuck in our old ways and are not prepared to stop controlling and start surrendering. Surrendering the outcome and owning our reactions and our roles in situations can bring us great freedom, but this requires faith. We need to believe in things unseen, that the universe or some other higher power has our backs, or that things will be okay. We need to believe that we can ride the wave.

The cool thing is that transformation doesn't have to be big. It's happening in the day-to-day moments. As you find new learnings, your evolution is moving forward. You are being flawsome.

What beliefs about myself do I keep defending that might have some truth to them?

_____

_____

_____

_____

_____

_____

_____

_____

_____

8

It's an Inside Job

Wouldn't it be great if we could outsource our evolution to someone else? We could do a contra deal: I'll look after your kids if you go and do *my* work—my emotional work, I mean. (Actually, I think I'd rather do the emotional work than look after someone else's kids; I reckon it's because I'm no longer afraid of the emotional work.) Yes, the emotional work is tough, and it can be daunting when you're at the beginning of your transformation. But trust me: there is always a reward on the other side when you take responsibility for your "stuff" and push through the discomfort.

Will You Accept?

Acceptance—particularly self-acceptance—is hard. But if you want to be flawsome, it's essential to accept all parts of yourself so you can either make peace with them or work on them. If you don't accept yourself, you will be in a constant struggle between denial and resistance: denying that certain characteristics are part of who you are or pushing the difficult parts of yourself away rather than trying to understand them.

In his book *The War of Art* (highly recommended reading), Steven Pressfield describes resistance like this:

> Resistance cannot be seen, touched, heard, or smelled. But it can be felt. We experience it as an energy field radiating from a work-in-potential. It's a repelling force. It's negative. Its aim is to shove us away, distract us, prevent us from doing our work. Resistance is always lying and always full of shit.

Resistance gets in the way of our evolution. It blocks us from creating peace within ourselves, getting that project done, finishing that book (yep, I know it), repairing that relationship, and owning our triggers. You can't beat a river into submission; you need to surrender to its current. Just like a river, you have a current, a rhythm that is unique to you. It doesn't mean you will always be that way, but the sooner you recognize your rhythm and know it to be true, the easier your transformation will be.

When I was writing this book, wildfires were ravaging my country of Australia. I had been having a discussion with a relative about the reason we'd seen such unprecedented damage. He didn't believe in climate change. I wanted to understand his thinking and find out what information he based his decision on. Apparently, the newspaper told him. I asked him if he had entertained the idea that some journalists and media organizations have their own agendas and perhaps their reporting could be a little biased. He insisted that all reporters tell the truth.

I could see how he had formed this opinion, and I let him know this. I then asked him if he would be up for reading a well-written, fact-driven article about climate change. He refused. I suggested that maybe I could read some of the articles he sided with and we could have a discussion about our different perspectives. But no, he wasn't interested.

This got me thinking. Why was he so adamant about not even entertaining another perspective? Whether it's climate change, who we vote for, how we bring up our kids, religion, or even how to pack the dishwasher, why do we get so stuck in our views and our need to defend our positions, no matter what? We all have opinions on things we don't know enough about; that's not new. But why do we refuse to budge on topics that we are passionate about?

Could it be that we are scared to consider another perspective in case we discover that our thinking is wrong, misinformed, or flawed? That we would need to concede that we're wrong and that this might challenge our sense of self? If we believe that what we stand for is who we are or that our opinions determine our characters, then being wrong could seem to be a sign that our characters are flawed. If we have been comfortable thinking about an issue in a certain way and are faced with evidence that we are wrong, our egos might be too self-protected to admit it.

> **Acceptance is hard, yet that's how we grow.**

Is it too hard to accept that your thinking might be flawed because you are human? Acceptance is hard, yet that's how we grow. What things are you resisting in your life now? Friends, work issues, decisions, conversations? If you change your mind, what would it mean for you?

What are you struggling to accept about yourself that is creating resistance?

_____

_____

_____

_____

_____

_____

_____

_____

_____

_____

_____

_____

_____

_____

_____

_____

_____

_____

_____

Learn to Be with You

I was in an Uber the other day when I noticed the driver was taking the long way to get me home. *Grrr.* I could feel my hands tensing and my jaw tightening. My body was telling me I was stressed. As soon as I feel tension in my body, I know I am resisting something.

Learning to read your own signs of stress, resistance, or tension is essential. It means you can decide how to act next. I had a choice: I could leave the driver to follow his map or ask him to go the way I knew was faster. But to make this decision, I first needed to be present enough to notice my body was feeling tense. I needed to be with *me.*

You can't hear when you are always hustling.

Are you a busy person? Do you always have something to do? Does it feel like you will never get to properly rest? In the last few years, I have really challenged myself about what I *have* to do and what I *choose* to do. Busy people always have something they *need* to do because no one else can do it as well as them. Often our being busy is a result of us feeling as though we are not "enough." It's hard to observe our bodies and hear the truth when we are in this space; it's like trying to hear voices in a tsunami.

We live in a society that places value on doing stuff, being something, achieving success. If we did everything our world told us we "need" to, we would be exhausted. The good thing is, we get to choose. Our value to others diminishes when we can't be present; we are doing, not being. When we practice stillness, allowing ourselves to feel our emotions, that's when the magic can happen. We need to learn to just *be* with ourselves.

By the way, I ended up politely asking the Uber driver about the directions his app had suggested. He agreed that the app didn't always suggest the best way, and we both had the same idea of how to travel there faster. All that tension I felt I allowed for no reason.

Connect with Something Other Than Yourself

When our lives are bigger than just ourselves, they become better. We become happier, more joyful, and less selfish. Why is this important when it comes to finding your flawsome? Because learning about yourself can be hard work; connecting with others can help you feel supported and less alone while you're going through this learning.

David Brooks, political commentator for the *New York*

Times, found himself in a space of deep loneliness after experiencing a marriage breakdown and rifts between himself and his friends due to his work. After reflecting, he came up with three lies that weren't serving him:

1. **Career success is fulfilling.** (The lie of success.) Brooks had achieved "success," but he realized he threw himself into work to avoid the shame he felt underneath. Achieving career success became a way to hide how he really felt about himself.
2. **I can make myself happy.** (The lie of self-sufficiency.) Brooks realized that we can't do everything for ourselves, that independence isn't always something to be celebrated, especially if it creates distance between ourselves and others.
3. **I am what I have achieved.** (The lie of meritocracy.) Brooks concluded that our assumptions that people who have achieved more are worth more just make us keep chasing our tails (or the tails of others).

When he was not reaching out to others—to connect, to articulate his loneliness and his sense of loss—Brooks felt worse. This is probably true for many of us. My research for this book proves it too: nearly 75 percent of the people I interviewed said that when they are in a dark place, they nearly always distance themselves from others, or they keep their company but do not reveal their true thoughts. Most of my interviewees recognized that this did not serve them, but the shame they felt about revealing themselves prevented them from connecting.

Brooks says we are in a "social and relational crisis." I think he's right. We are better at disconnection than connection. The irony of social media is that it was created for us to connect, yet it draws us inside—not outside. We post pictures of our "happy" lives and create unrealistic expectations for others. It is a platform for keyboard warriors to judge, not listen. Instead of spending time together, in person, we have become digital pen pals.

Show me a happy person who lives in isolation of others. Show me someone who has made a life without other humans and has joy. We are wired to connect.

What am I doing that's getting in the way of my own evolution?

_____

_____

_____

_____

_____

_____

_____

_____

_____

_____

_____

_____

_____

_____

Walk Away to Find Yourself

Winnie-the-Pooh, the fictional bear created by A. A. Milne in the early 1920s, is known to say that he always gets to where he is going by walking away from where he has been. Now that's a smart bear! What does "walking away from where you've been" mean? And how does it help?

Those who have read or watched *Into the Wild* might be picturing themselves venturing alone into the wilderness, but walking away to find yourself does not need to have such a dramatic intention. It's about walking away from things that don't serve you, away from things that keep you below the line. It could mean walking away from people in your life who keep you gossiping or who create tension and drama. It could mean walking away from a job or company that your values don't align with. Or it could mean walking away from beliefs, assumptions, and opinions that keep you from learning.

Walking away is about surrendering to things unknown and having faith in things you can't see. It's sitting in the unknown rather than trying to control your environment or the people around you. When you walk away, you recognize that you can be more present when you no longer cling to ideals, opinions, assumptions, and truths that don't serve you.

To recalibrate, we often need to pull back; like a slingshot, we can be more powerful the further we pull back. But if we go too far, the slingshot will snap. We need to know the difference between pulling back and escaping. They can look the same but come from very different intents.

Einstein reportedly said that "no problem can be solved from the same consciousness that created it." We have to expand our minds and our hearts to be able to tackle the issues in our lives. Today's problems can't be solved by yesterday's solutions. Sometimes we need to step away from our former thinking patterns to step into ourselves. We need to give ourselves permission to be exactly as we are, for now. If we are not prepared to do this, we can remain trapped—and our flaws will be the focus, rather than acceptance.

What could I walk away from that isn't serving me?

9

Pick Your Pain

According to the author of *Man's Search for Meaning*, Viktor Frankl, we can find meaning in life in three ways:

1. In close, loving relationships
2. In service to others
3. In pain

The first two make sense, but pain? It might seem strange to think that things that torment, distress, or wound us or cause discomfort could create meaning for us. But stick with me here.

Let's look at relationships. Have you ever found yourself in friendships or even romantic relationships that don't serve you? It could be that you're always the one who ends up taking responsibility for the smooth running of the household, or you always end up being friends with people who don't appreciate you. At work, do you notice any patterns? Do you seem to always wind up with a passive-aggressive boss, a job that requires lots of overtime, or coworkers who talk behind your back? What about parenting? Is your child driving you mad? Does he or she show little respect?

None of these scenarios are enjoyable. They cause pain, stress, anxiety, and suffering—especially when we seem to keep repeating them. To cope with these issues, we tend to go into denial about the role we play or develop self-destructive behaviors to reduce the stress.

What if we are trying to avoid the pain of the whole truth (yours and theirs)? If we see repeated patterns of difficult situations occurring in our lives, couldn't it be us that is the common denominator? But instead of owning that pain, we make the situation mean something else—something that is easier for us to reconcile. These are the stories we tell ourselves about others, the assumptions we make.

Transformation and learning are available to us in these situations, yet we give the gold away. We ask others to change or simply blame them instead of identifying the parts of ourselves that don't serve us.

So we have a choice: We can choose to experience the pain

of staying the same, making similar mistakes time after time and staying in the same holding pattern in life. Or we can choose the pain of growth. We can accept our flaws, knowing we can think and behave below the line. Growth is about learning and evolving. Suffering holds great power when we navigate it wisely.

Learn to Struggle Well

The mother of one of my best friends has been married three times. All three relationships ended painfully. Her husbands either died or cheated on her. Yet while she was experiencing grief and loss, she looked truly fabulous. She always made sure she didn't look how she felt; she dressed well, put her "face" on, and did her hair beautifully. When people told her she looked amazing, she would respond, "I know, darling. Misery suits me." I gotta say, I love her and her attitude to bits. She knew pain; she didn't avoid it or deny it. She learned how to push through it. A warrior knows a battle will be tough. A business owner knows there will be painful times. A parent knows it's not all roses. My friend's mom learned how to struggle well.

I've received the gift of a broken heart a few times now. Yep, I call it a gift. The pain of being in the wrong relationship is one thing. Learning from it is the gift. This means that the next time a relationship doesn't work out and I end up hurt, I will struggle through the pain better than last time. If one relationship doesn't work, I can't go to the next one thinking it will automatically be different. I am the same person, so there is a chance that it could work out in a similar way to last time—unless I have learned from the experience.

Even those who have experienced the pain of what I call *dirty trauma*—heartbreak so intense that it throws you to the ground and kicks you in the guts and feels like it has no end—have choices after this experience. You can either build up your walls and go back to denial and blame, or you can work through it. You can figure out the role you played (without self-flagellation) and the learnings you can take from the experience and come back a little stronger and wiser (and more flawsome).

Pain left undealt with doesn't change; it just takes another form. In an episode of his podcast *Under the Skin*, Russell Brand talked with Brené Brown about the saying, "Pain not transformed will become pain transmitted." They discussed how if we are not aware when we are suffering, we cause others to suffer as well. We stay in blame, denial, and resentment toward others and life; we become joyless; we don't listen or accept advice; we are broken.

But if you are broken open, pain becomes a gift. It gives you the opportunity to experience growth.

Becoming flawsome means having the courage to see our

flaws, accept them, and know they might require some work. Courage is accepting feedback or trying on a different truth or perspective. Courage is owning the impact you have on others. Courage is knowing you may have caused others pain.

We can't avoid the struggle, but we can decide how we want to do it.

Pain Grows in the Dark

Think about something in your life that you have either never shared with anyone or held on to for a long time. It could be something that happened to you, something you did that you were not proud of, a lie you told, a secret you kept for another person that needed to be aired, or a belief you hold that you have not shared. It has caused you pain to hold on to it, but the fear of sharing it was so strong you stayed where you were and kept it in. We call this *shame*. It's beyond being embarrassed; it's when we don't feel worthy because of this unspoken thing. It makes us feel dirty, not good enough, flawed, or flat-out wrong. The thing about shame is that it hides; it stays in the dark so no one else can see it. We think if we hide it, it also means we don't have to look at it or think about it ourselves. We try to keep it there as long as we can so we can continue with our everyday lives.

If we keep things in the dark, they are still *there*; they haven't gone away. And because we have not aired them, talked them out, or worked through what is true and not true, we don't have any perspective. We unknowingly make things bigger and stronger, giving them power over us.

Let's look at something relatively small: little white lies. It's easy to see why outright lying or deception can cause suffering, because you know in your head and heart that you're being sneaky and malicious. But what about the impact of those little ones—the ones that you might even have told with good intent, because you *don't* want to hurt someone?

White lies can affect your mental health because they keep you in a charade. White lies aren't just said to others; we tell them to ourselves. They're like a mask that prevents us from discussing the real issue. They can lead to our own anxiety and stress, especially if one white lie leads to another. People hear your content but smell your intent, right? So white lies disconnect you from others, because they can sense your integrity might be a bit off but they can't prove it. They can also disconnect you from yourself. Lies can affect your sleep and your own trust issues with others. If you can't trust yourself, how can you trust someone else?

Withholding the truth and replacing it with a false one can cause us to feel ashamed—of our own deception and the tension it creates within ourselves. Every truth we choose not to look at or listen to keeps us in the dark in some way and makes flawsome harder to reach. We can see our white lies as flaws rather than pain that just needs to be transformed.

Gabby Bernstein is a multiple bestselling author and speaker.

Her motto is "Be the happiest person you know." On her website gabbybernstein.com, she says:

> For the past fifteen years, I've been on stages in front of thousands of people sharing my truth. I've willingly spoken on behalf of unspoken shame, sharing stories of addiction, codependency, health conditions, infertility, mental illness, and trauma. Through these stories, I've healed myself and others. Sharing my truth openly has been a catalyst for growth in the world. But an interesting thing happens when you become brave enough to tell the truth. I like to refer to it as, "You go first." When we speak our truth, we go first so we can give others permission to recognize and share their truth.
>
> It's safer to shine a light on our shadows than it is to hide from them.

The hard thing about living in darkness is that you sometimes can't climb your way out by yourself. You need interdependence, where you learn to struggle with others and share your vulnerability in turn. The cycle is good for everyone; it's when community, friendship, and life work best. It's when everyone has permission to be flawsome and work through their stuff together.

> The parts of ourselves we want to hide from are likely to be the parts that need a light shined on them.

Where am I picking the pain of staying the same? What could the pain of growth look like?

_____

_____

_____

_____

_____

_____

10

Hold the Space for Flawsome

Can you hold the space for yourself to be flawsome—to accept that you are flawed and will think and behave both below and above the line? Can you be okay with accepting the good parts as well as the things you're not so proud of? An athlete knows that most days they will wake up in pain; they create space for that. Why can't we?

Can you hold the space for the things you've said and done that you feel bad about or the truths you've kept in the dark? Can you air out those lies, big or small? Can you admit to yourself that you are not always awesome—that you fail at stuff (but you're not a failure)? If you treat someone poorly, can you own that but realize you're not a bad person overall? Can you be brave enough to admit to yourself, and to others, that you have work to do on yourself? That you are a normal, flawed, sometimes triggered, defensive, retreating, unhelpful, sometimes selfish human? I can—not always in the moment but at least afterward.

> **I am un-wedding myself from this ridiculous notion that I am not allowed to fail.**

I've learned, and I am still learning, to hold the space to think about it, look at it, question it, acknowledge it, and own it. I know that facing up to my flaws will feel bad. I will feel guilty, even ashamed. But I will work to move through, because if I don't allow myself the time and space to acknowledge my flaws, I am picking the pain of staying the same. I don't know about you, but I'd rather pick the pain of evolution so at least I'm being productive.

Awareness Creates Breakthroughs

At some stage, we need to break the automatic cycle of responding to our triggers. If we can't see our responses, we are not able to shift them. If we are not able to see our triggers in the moment, we will respond as we always have—as our bodies know and our minds are used to.

In his book *Stop Missing Your Life,* my friend Cory Muscara tells us that being human is hard. He says that if we can become more aware of what we see, feel, experience, and think, then we can move forward.

Muscara is an expert in mindfulness. I've read a lot of books on the art of mindfulness, and I love his description a lot:

> This is not about meditation. This is about intentionally moving closer to our human experience, learning how to dance with it, to be at peace with it—maybe even enjoy it. It's not about clearing your mind. It's about developing an awareness of what is going on in our mind and being intentional about where we direct it. The day, from start to finish, is a playground for presence.

Muscara teaches us that simply being courageous enough to see and notice what is going on and how we are reacting allows us to develop the internal freedom and growth that we were destined to have.

Awareness is something that we cultivate and tend. It's a

practice that requires *practice*. We need to learn how to create the space to do this—and this can be done ourselves, without paying thousands of dollars to experts.

How we experience triggers, truths, and moments will profoundly affect our responses. How we experience pain will allow us to move forward.

Can You Breathe?

Have you ever defragged your computer? *Defragmentation* is a process that helps computers access files on the hard drive faster. Just like your computer, you need to create space and time to reset how you think, feel, and be. Breathing helps us do this. I'm not referring to the regular breathing you are doing now; I mean the intentional, present kind of breathing that helps us relax into the present and stop focusing on the shame of the past and the anxiety of the future. In a way, breathing is about resetting our own internal files so we can see things clearly and access truths that will serve us. It enables us to search for the truth without escalating to fight or flight mode.

Breathing is powerful. It allows you to take a step back from whatever is bothering you. It expands your brain's capacity to think more clearly. In times of stress, it calms your nervous system.

> **Breathing can be your superpower.**

Right now, I want you to try this. I want you to breathe through your nose. Breathe in for three slow counts. Hold for three counts. Breathe out for three. Hold for three. Do this two more times.

What have you noticed? Did you feel your body relax just a little? Did your mind become a little less cluttered? Were you more conscious of where you were lying or sitting? Did you sit up more or relax more?

Breathing works. It helps us connect to ourselves and hold the space for where we are at. We just need to learn to do it mindfully to help us be in the moment.

What do I need to be mindful of right now about my flaws?

_____

_____

_____

_____

_____

_____

11

Get Stuck in Growth

As we've discussed, we can choose the pain of staying the same or the pain of growth. For me, it's a no-brainer: I choose growth. I am committed to my own evolution. Will I miss opportunities to do this? *Abso-friggin-lutely.* I am human. I might intentionally miss growth opportunities, or it could happen subconsciously. What I want to be able to do is evolve so I no longer feel triggered when I am with myself, with others, and making my way through the world. Will there be a time when I am never triggered? That's a big, fat *no* from me. I am not prepared to do that much work. I am okay with the pace of my evolution, for now.

Controlling my reactions to respond well requires short-term control. Evolving so I am triggered less often is long term.

FORGIVE YOUR DAMN SELF

Growth takes time, but if you're committed to it, you will be surprised to find you're evolving in ways you never thought possible.

Know This: You Will Disappoint Others

As I touched on earlier, in 2019, I leveled up in my career. I was offered a leadership role in which I would be involved in helping shape an organization and would work with people I love. I was excited. But with a new role comes new expectations—from yourself and, I soon learned, from those around you. The more responsibility you have, the more people expect of you. I knew the colleagues I was working with; we had worked together before, but not to this extent and not with me in my new leadership role.

After some time in this role, I learned that some of my colleagues had shared some feedback about me with our CEO. It wasn't all joy, love, and unicorns; there were words in there like "dismissive," "aggressive," and worst of all, "dangerous." These words came from people I trusted, valued, and respected. Thus, they *hurt*. I was upset that people saw me that way and that they didn't feel comfortable or even safe with me. The worst part was that I had really been working on myself; I thought I was starting to nail the self-awareness and become much more mindful of the impact I had on others.

I went digging for examples of when and where I had made people feel this way. A couple of situations were recent, a few occurred years ago, and some people had no examples at all—it was just how they felt.

So I had choices.

- ► I could reject the feedback and deny its truth.
- ► I could be offended and blame people who couldn't provide solid examples.
- ► I could be pissed off that people were talking about me behind my back.
- ► I could search for the real truth and take ownership of the role I played in others' experiences of me.
- ► I could forgive people for talking about me rather than to me.
- ► I could forgive myself for treating people as I did.
- ► I could learn from it all so next time I could see or feel myself about to do the same thing, I would be able to pull back.

What did I choose? A bit of all of them, to be honest. I started in denial: "I am not that person." I moved to being mildly offended that people didn't come to me. (Although I moved on from this way of thinking quickly, because I know why people didn't come to me; I get it—I've written two books on feedback.)

I took responsibility for what I said and did, and I came to an understanding of how others felt. I am proud I moved into forgiveness. I called those whom I had wronged; I apologized and thanked them for sharing their experience. Then I did the harder one: I forgave myself.

This situation was a pivotal moment for me. It reminded me that when you think *I've evolved*, the irony of life shows you that there is no such space. I learned that I will always disappoint people; it's in my nature and nurture. I learned that I have a choice about how I respond and rewire. Once again, how people treat you is a measure of their character; how you respond is a measure of yours.

You will let people down, whether it's via something you did or did not do or something you had no idea would impact others. That doesn't mean you need to live in disappointment. As Dita Von Teese says, "You can be the juiciest, ripest peach in the world and there's still going to be people who hate peaches."

Rewrite Your Beliefs

For over fifteen years, I have been drawn to a memory I have of my ninth birthday party. We were playing pass the parcel. Mum was making sure the parcel went around fast enough and that everyone got a hold. Dad was on the music. Mum had wrapped the parcel with a little gift inside each layer so that everyone got a present when the music stopped. It hadn't stopped on me yet. The parcel was getting smaller and smaller. Finally, the music stopped for the last time—not on me. I can't remember what the final gift was or what happened straight after, but the next thing I knew, I was in my bedroom with the door shut. I had been told that if I was going to act like a spoiled brat, I could go to my room.

You might be thinking, *But, Georgia, it was your birthday— you had probably already received dozens of presents.* Yes, I know. But that feeling I had in my bedroom has never left me: I felt really alone.

This memory has come up so many times for me, and it wasn't until last year that I understood why. I attended a healing ministry, with three ladies who are experienced in the art of helping people move through past pain. Now, I had no idea what was going to come up in that session. I thought it might help me deal with my mum and dad stuff or past lost loves or broken friendships. (Yep, I was creating expectations again rather than being outcome agnostic.)

The ladies asked what memory was coming up, and I reluctantly told them about my birthday party. They helped me to relive the moment, as if I were back in my room, crying and feeling so alone. They asked me what I believed in that moment. It was then that I realized it had nothing to do with not getting a present. In that moment, I had decided two things about myself: that *I am too needy* and that *I will always be on my own.*

Now the floodgates of shame tears were opening. We talked about the areas of my life in which these beliefs have played out in negative ways. I realized that, for most of my life, I had walked in these beliefs. I have always believed that I am the needy one in relationships and that I will always be alone.

> **I got to rewrite my beliefs that day. I walk lighter now.**

Most of the time, I do not believe people see me as needy (although I am still working on this). I know I am not on my own. How I live has changed. When someone in my personal life doesn't return a call or cancels a catch-up, I don't try to make that mean anything other than what it is. In the past, I would sometimes think people did that because I ask too much of them, but now I know this is not so.

When I get close to people, I am now less concerned about whether it will go somewhere further. Rumi was right:

> Your task is not to seek love, but merely to seek
> and find all the barriers within yourself that you
> have built against it.

It now makes sense why this memory kept coming up: I needed to process it. My faulty beliefs dictated how I connected with others. Our childhood memories are strong and powerful, but our beliefs about them are often untrue. We just need to find ways to work through them and be prepared to go to the difficult places in our minds.

Forgiveness Is Your Growth Pill

When Tyra Banks was called a "super-waddle," she had choices. She could have resented the press, taken it personally, and felt rejected—both physically and emotionally. She could have gone on a media rant to criticize the critics. She could have taken the feedback on board and let it define her sense of self. (After all, her career was all about looking fabulous.) But she didn't. She rose strong.

She turned the experience into an opportunity, because she is a professional. Professionals know that others will be haters, others will criticize, others will blame. They know they have a choice about what they take on board and learn from and what they dismiss. They don't make it personal. They treat criticism with compassion and forgiveness: compassion for self, forgiveness for others.

The thing about forgiveness is that it's not a gift for another. It's a gift for ourselves. Forgiveness helps *us* move forward so we can stop the cycle of pain transferred from one to another.

Forgiveness is not easy. It can take time, but it should be carried out on our own terms. We need to be patient with ourselves and accept that it can be a slow process. In his book *The Mastery of Self*, Don Miguel Ruiz Jr. says:

> Respecting yourself also means being honest with yourself. If you are not ready to forgive, that is your truth. Don't subjugate yourself with "I have to." If you are not ready, you are not ready; and the acceptance of yourself with this truth is practicing unconditional love… Forgiving is the final step of healing a wound.

We just need to know that the battle in our heads will continue until we can move to a place of forgiveness. Awareness of this is key.

We are not perfect. People will tell us so, because that's their truth. We don't have to make it ours or be offended by it. Dropping offense and stepping into compassion—forgiving others for the words or actions that triggered us—is above the line. Forgiving *ourselves* is evolution. We are often our own worst critics. We are experts in punishing ourselves.

You are likely to have to keep taking the forgiveness pill. Sometimes daily, sometimes hourly. We do life with flawsome people. We make mistakes often. It's okay. We can forgive and be forgiven.

I constantly need to forgive myself for putting my (unwarranted and not asked for) opinions on others. I'd love others to forgive me for doing so. Luckily, my friends are gracious; they know my heart. Unless of course I've pushed it too hard. My friend Annie will give me *the face*; I have learned that I have overstepped the mark when I see this. The more I am aware of the role I play and the more I forgive myself for it, the less I do it. Mindfulness works. Who would have thunk it?

Have a meeting with yourself, and see what needs to be on your forgiveness agenda. Percolate in it. You may not have deserved whatever you've been on the receiving end of, yet you have a choice about how you respond. You can be bigger than the experience. Your destiny is not to walk around holding grudges against others or yourself. That was never the plan.

Find Your Superpower

My friend Callum McKirdy is flawsome. Callum is one of those guys who everybody loves. He's endearing, kind, funny, and thoughtful. He's all about the people he is with. And like most humans, he doesn't see himself like we see him. But that's changing.

He's in the process of making his flaws his superpowers. For his whole life, Callum has struggled with things that most of us take for granted—such as filling in forms, using ATMs, shopping online, or using e-kiosks. He's a competent facilitator, mentor, and speaker, but some other tasks were always hard. And instead of articulating that, he would hide it. He would create ways to cope with it rather than share it with those around him.

It wasn't until 2019, when he was diagnosed with ADHD and dyslexia, that he realized how much energy and time he spent on trying to do "normal" things. It wasn't the diagnosis itself that was significant; it was being able to give a name to the things that held him back. He can now see that the way he lived his life held him back and created self-limiting beliefs.

Callum says:

> Let me be clear—neither dyslexia nor ADHD
> are disabilities; they're naturally occurring

neuro types that happen to be a minority. The western world has been established on norms defined by the majority, which is why systems are more difficult for neuro-divergent people to cope with and adapt to. Education, the internet, commerce, etc., have been designed for the beer belly of the bell curve, not the extremes.

Callum doesn't wear his diagnosis as an excuse; it's just allowed him to understand himself. He calls himself "ADHD positive." I love this so much. The cool thing is that he has used who he is and molded it into his superpower. He has surrendered to it and allowed himself to be flawsome. Callum says:

I've now found a niche for myself helping leaders uncover, unlock, and unleash their potential—the difference and uniqueness of their collective group. I can now help others harness the power of people with different minds and ways of doing things. I've found my place using the superpowers often characterized by neurodiverse thinkers.

He is an example of ownership without it being an excuse. He's not the guy who says, "I can't do that because I have ADHD." He hasn't made it his identity; it's just a way to understand himself. For the first time in his life, he says he knows who he is now. He's no longer an outcast.

Who we are—our characteristics, personalities, physical selves, and wholeness—is our superpower. The challenge is in connecting to it (not being triggered by it), surrendering to it (finding the truth in it), and letting it evolve (the transformation). We all have the opportunity to do this.

I have always been a little bit obsessed with female superheroes. When I was growing up, I loved the Bionic Woman (Jaime Sommers) and Xena the Warrior Princess (a New Zealand icon). I also had an extraspecial place in my heart for Wonder Woman. I was fascinated by her Lasso of Truth: all she needed to do was put her lasso around someone, and they were compelled to tell the truth. That was her superpower.

Imagine if we had our own Lasso of Truth for ourselves. Our lasso could cut through the fears, the shame, and the assumptions we make about ourselves and just get to the bottom of it. The good thing is, even without a lasso, we all have the power to rewrite the truth about our supposed flaws. We can turn them into our superpowers, if we dare.

Choose Useful Beliefs over Limiting Ones

In 2019, my son, Jacko, was studying high level math in eleventh grade. Toward the end of the year, he decided not to hand in his final project for media studies and instead put his energy into the two math exams—since these would count toward his final school score.

I found out that he didn't hand in his final project via an email from his teacher. Jacko had decided to rely on the "ask for forgiveness, not permission" theory. If he had subscribed to the rules of school, he would have had to hand the project in because the school said it was part of his Year 11 results (and rightly so). But Jacko decided that wasn't a good enough reason or the best use of this time.

I am not advocating rebellion here, but I am open to a good argument. Jacko is not defined by what the school thinks; he's nearly an adult and living by his own rules. The thing is, we all have access to amazing teachers, past and present, these days via the wonderful world of the internet: Gandhi, Brené Brown, Thich Nhat Hanh, Barack and Michelle Obama, Nelson Mandela, Maya Angelou, Jay Shetty, and more. There are many who offer great advice about a smarter, happier, better way to do life. The cool thing is that we get to choose to listen and act on their advice or not. That's the great thing about having a free will, right? Yet as we lose our innocent mindset, we often fall into the trap of living by rules that don't serve us.

As kids, we run around naked in the grass with the sprinklers on, we wear clothes that don't match, we say things that don't make sense, and we talk to strangers like we know them. Then, as we grow into our adolescence, we become conscious of the world we live in, the world that creates "rules" around how we should dress, eat, dance, work, and hold our knife and fork. And we believe them. We believe ads on social media that our teeth are not white enough; a sexual partner says we should really be more open to exploring things, so we decide we need to do that. We choose to believe these rules so we can be enough—not just for ourselves but for everyone else. This is where we form an image of perfection.

The authors of *The Fifth Agreement* propose that we are perfect as we are. It's our beliefs that we picked up along the way that get in the way of us believing this. We believe the saying "No one's perfect." I say "Pffft, we are." We just don't know how to believe it yet. We are blinded by the lies we have been told about what perfection is.

Like Jacko, we can create new rules that serve our purpose better. We just need to keep in mind we have to live with the consequences and think about whether they will hurt others around us.

Oh, and, Jacko, thanks for the reminder. Maybe just give me a heads-up before your teacher emails me next time.

Pick one belief that you would like to rewrite into a superpower. What could you turn it in to?

The Big (Little) Finish

Your quest doesn't finish here. Nor did it start when you first opened this book: it's been ongoing since you were born. The next move is up to you, so ask yourself: *What stories am I telling myself that no longer serve me? How am I hiding from the truth?*

Remember: to be flawsome involves not just accepting your flaws but also understanding where they come from. It's not just making peace with your flaws; it's knowing that without them, you would not be you. It's about giving yourself permission to be you. So don't make information the enemy: you give your power away that way. You have the power to choose whether you would rather feel the pain of staying the same or the pain of transformation.

What is your choice? Would you rather seek the truth and work through your pain and triggers so you can gain a true understanding of yourself and your experiences? Or are you going to stay in blame, denial, resentment, and mistrust?

> **Transformation lies in the courage to choose discomfort and take responsibility for yourself and the impact you may have on those around you.**

It's as simple as noticing your triggers. See them. Name them. Take responsibility for them. They are yours. Seek the truth. Be open to many perspectives. Don't take differing ideas, people, or situations personally.

The simplicity of it all is that transformation comes from inside. It's not a place you need to go to. It's just a matter of finding the gold.

To finish, I will leave you with one of the most beautiful statements by Elisabeth Kübler-Ross. Elisabeth was a Swiss-American psychiatrist, recognized in *Time* magazine as one of the "100 Most Important Thinkers" of the twentieth century. She is well known for her expertise in grief, which led to development of the Kübler-Ross grief model. It's been used globally for nearly forty years. She said:

> The most beautiful people we have known are those who have known defeat, known suffering, known struggle, known loss, and have found their way out of the depths. These persons have an appreciation, a sensitivity, and an understanding of life that fills them with compassion, gentleness, and deep loving concern.

Elisabeth understood that pain needs to be moved through, that it's a process. If we don't allow the process to unfold and deal with what arises, we can become stuck. When we don't recognize and own our triggers, we become stuck. We pick the pain of staying the same.

My hope for you is that you are able to learn from this book, that you become committed to your evolution while knowing you have flaws and there will always be work to do. I hope you can know that this is enough.

You have the power to be flawsome, just as you are. You just need to choose to accept this.

How can you step into making peace with who you are and owning all your flawsomeness?

Acknowledgments

They say it takes a village to raise a child. Well, it takes a tribe to be able to do life with energy and resolve, and my tribe is the best there is. Just sayin'.

Annie and James, you provided the place for me, and for many, to start reconciling this whole flawsome journey. To learn that who we are, as we are, is enough. You pioneered something new in a community that was stuck in old ways. So much love and respect to you both.

Peter Cook, you are a general, a five-star, a great friend, and divine mentor. Your ability to teach much with few words is remarkable—something we could all aspire to. My practice and my character are better because of you.

Lesley Williams, my publisher, it's been smooth sailing

from the beginning. What an easy ride to go on. Thank you. And Brooke Lyons, my editor, thanks for "getting me" from the beginning and letting my voice shine through.

To the tribe I do life with, you know who you are. I would not be me without you. You have accepted me as I am. You have consistently given me permission to be flawsome and shown me I am awesome regardless. You don't let me hide. You never let me fall. You are the best group of humans a gal could ever know. If we were an army, we would never be defeated.

To those who might not feel I'm their cup of tea, thank you. Thank you for allowing me to see my triggers. My learnings here have often been my greatest.

To my kids, Holly and Jacko (if you ever read this), you have both taught me so much. You have allowed me to see my whole self through parenting. As you grow older, the roles are reversed and I am now learning from you (and loving it). I am excited to grow with you and grateful you've chosen to stay so close to your dear ol' ma.

About Georgia

Georgia is not a conventional human. She's a little left of center, a self-defined "quirky corporate." Her background is also atypical. She has led people and culture, marketing, sales and business development, and recruitment. She initially started as an accountant. Go figure!

The one constant in Georgia's global career has been her determination to ensure we all have real conversations—the ones we need to have with each other, including *about* each other. Her work in this space has led her to be recognized as Australia's leading expert in designing feedback cultures. She has authored two bestselling books about this: *Fixing Feedback* and *Feedback Flow*.

Georgia has worked with some of the best teams and organizations around the world including Atlassian, Telstra, Dior, Australia Post, Canva, Airtasker, the University of Melbourne, MYOB, BP, and many more. She has learned that the key to any successful team is people: when they are at their best, the business is too.

Georgia is a keynote speaker, facilitator, trainer, and mentor in strategic planning and workforce culture. Her MO is helping people make peace with who they are. She is a single mum to her teenagers, Jacko and Holly, and lives in bayside Melbourne.

She's an avid yogi, a dinner party lover, and a self-confessed excellent reverse parker. She barely speaks French.

Visit georgiamurch.com to find out more and subscribe to Georgia's blogs to see what she is thinking about lately. You can also find her on Instagram, Facebook, and LinkedIn.